MASTER THE MINDSET OF AN ENTREPRENEUR

THE PERFECT BLEND OF RIGHT MINDSET & ENTREPRENEURSHIP

MRUDHULA RAVI KIRAN

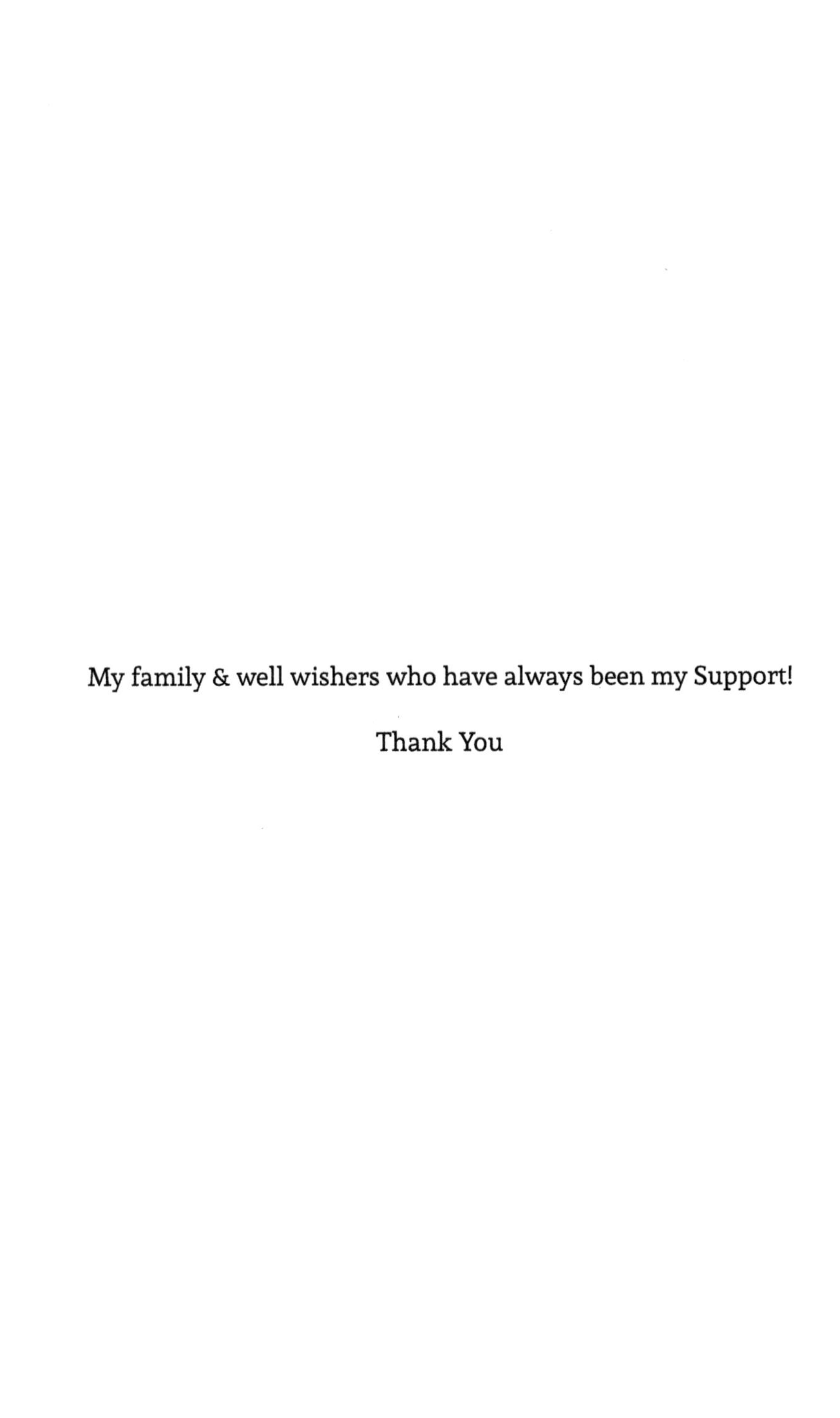

My family & well wishers who have always been my Support!

Thank You

Contents

Contents

MASTER

THE

MINDSET

OF AN

ENTREPRENEUR

THE PERFECT BLEND OF RIGHT MINDSET & ENTREPRENEURSHIP

MRUDHULA RAVI KIRAN

PREFACE

It takes an immense amount of dedication and strong mindset to even think about becoming an ENTREPRENEUR!

The path that we take as an Entrepreneur has a beauty of its own!

Every profession or every phase of life is submerged with challenges, no job or profession is a piece of cake to walk through.

The only difference of being an Entrepreneur is –

YOU OWN YOUR BUSINESS!

YOU ARE THE MASTER OF YOUR BUSINESS!

Find the best traits that equip you to face the challenges as an optimist, find the proven techniques that turn the problems into opportunities, know the power of your Mind.

Mind is amazing but we have been in the impression of restricting it with some limitations. But, it is possible to find a way to frame our Goals, understand our capabilities and

NOW It's Time to wake YOUR BEST VERSION!

MIND IS THE BEST GIFT!

Mrudhula Ravi Kiran

I

Introduction

"The true test of an Entrepreneur is how efficiently one can handle his/her business during the time of Crisis"

Welcome to the journey of Right Mindset Transformation!

Let's begin with a thank you, for being born and for being alive in this super fast digital era, where every task is possible with super fast paced-technology within the reach of our finger-tips.

The most important aspect is to train ourselves to stay updated and upgraded with the current trend has become mandatory.

With this busy schedule of constant research to level up our thoughts and energy, we sometimes tend to forget that we are already gifted with inbuilt talent! It's just that we need to spend some quality time to discover and un-wrap this unique pre-loaded talent within us.

DID YOU KNOW THAT MIND IS THE BEST GIFT WE CAN EVER ASK FOR!
IT IS THE BIGGEST ASSET FOR THE MANKIND!

Before we dive deep into the concept of this Book, let's begin with the basic understanding of what does Mindset mean?

A Mindset is simply a belief – "A belief about you, your capabilities, qualities, personality and talents. What matters the most in terms of motivation is whether we see these abilities as a Gift for Growth or Fixed for life.

We know that an Entrepreneur or Entrepreneurship is an important driving force for economic growth and industrial transformation and also for the growth of employment opportunities.

There are numerous definitions revolving around the traits, characteristics, behavioural pattern and so on. But the Entrepreneurship does not depend on specific training or even a mandatory set of experiences. After all, there are business leaders with the most varied profiles and professional backgrounds, right? However, there are common points among successful entrepreneurs.

Let's begin to know more about these various factors responsible in the process of becoming the Master of your Mind that can impact tremendously on your business carrying it towards the path of Success.

NEW MINDSET
NEW RESULTS!

WHAT IS AN ENTREPRENEURIAL MINDSET?

Did you know that mindset directly influences our success or failure?

Maybe you've heard about mindset, but do you know what you can do to improve yours?

At first glance, it may seem like something very complicated, but believe me, it is possible to understand this concept and change your mental configuration once and for all, for better results, in all areas of your life.

DID YOU KNOW THAT THE COMBINATION OF:
THE RIGHT MINDSET & ENTREPRENEURSHIP CREATES WONDERS AND MIRACLES?

Mindset determines the way we face life, our goals, challenges, setbacks and difficulties, our performance, and how we strive to improve.

The entrepreneurial mindset can be defined as the mental adjustment necessary to achieve success as an entrepreneur.

It is totally related to emotional intelligence, because through emotional self-knowledge and emotional control it is possible to develop the mindset to undertake.

The entrepreneur needs to be self-motivated, recognize the emotional state of other people and have the ability to relate well.

A person with a right entrepreneurial mindset is one who can be courageous and realistic at the same time, evaluating every detail of the situation so as not to take unnecessary risks but take **CALCULATED** risk.

However, there will never be a completely safe scenario at every stage, yet the entrepreneur acts with courage to overcome adversity.

The great challenge lies in the fact that these aspects that form it are not apparent, as they are about thoughts and attitudes.

The good news is that even if you don't already have this vision, it can be developed with daily practice.

HOW DOES THE RIGHT MINDSET INFLUENCE ONE'S BUSINESS?

In simple words Mindset is to set up; it is the tuning of the mind. Our mind is like a computer with lots of software, some are good and some are bad.

How one sees the world, the aspects of personal and professional life is like a map formed by your beliefs and values.

Isn't it curious that two people have such different impressions of the same thing or event or a place?

For example: You go to an event with a co-worker. You say you liked the event and the ideas presented. However, your co-worker might disagree with the simple fact that, for him, the ideas were not interesting.

This is due to the mapping of each one's mind, the way to see the world is different. This map is made up of opinions, values and beliefs and governs the way we act on a daily basis.

"MINDSET IS THE LINE OF REASONING THAT DIRECT PEOPLE'S LIVES"

For example: You know the way to become a Millionaire, your mindset is tuned and you believe that you know it is possible and you also believe you will make it. But when you don't know this path, your mindset can be critical about it, even leading you to think it's impossible for you.

The Mindset is the perception of reality we have about ourselves! In other words, each one lives within their own reality. The reality that a millionaire lives is totally different from the reality that an initial stage beginner entrepreneur lives.

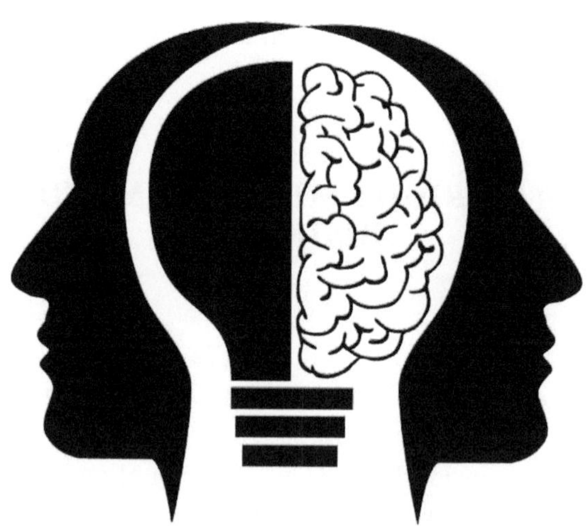

The Mindset that drives us varies from person to person. But it can be changed, that is, you can develop your Mindset to get into a new reality. The Mindset changes our life, as it is the way we see our reality that increases or decreases our belief in ourselves.

Have you ever thought about the importance of Mindset for your business and for you as an entrepreneur? You may have heard about it before, but you might have not given it much attention, as there might be other matters to worry about.

We are always busy, running out of time to be able to fulfil our daily obligations; sometimes we wish that the day has more than 24 hours due to the countless tasks. Most of us – the entrepreneurs would like to have a business running successfully and at the same time we wish to spend more quality time with our family and friends. We would like more financial peace of mind right?

For that to happen, you need to restructure your Mindset and influence everyone around you to do the same.

Improving the Mindset is the proven answer to gain productivity, dedicate more time to the family, deal better with your financial life and take care of yourself, not only with your work, but also with your appearance, in short - valuing self-esteem.

Each person is unique, so priorities are different. But there is something in common: everyone wants to develop their potential.

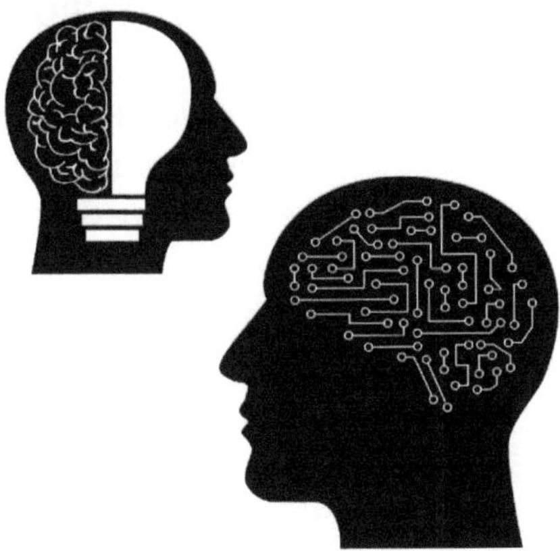

Changing our Mindset is easy as long as you know how to do it. You need to acquire new knowledge, read good books, and invest in relevant new courses.

Knowledge gives you wings, opens doors, transforms minds and attracts opportunities. The most important transformation that knowledge brings is that it makes us believe, when we know the path, we find it easier to believe that it is possible and that we have the capacity to do it.

The biggest challenge in gaining the right Mindset is we are often focused on changing somebody else's mindset rather than changing ours. We are often busy trying to change the mindset of the people around us.

A variety of reasons can lead someone to achieve the right Mindset.

Some people believe that people are born with the skills to succeed.

On the other hand, some develop the awareness that many things happen because of circumstances, these people are able to focus on their main objective and develop the skills they do not yet have. They are aware that learning is a process where there can be mistakes and failures; however, they are not shaken by the difficulties.

THEY DO NOT BYPASS CHALLENGES;
THEY SEEK TO LEARN FROM THEM
THAT'S THE MINDSET OF GROWTH

In this context, adopting a growth mindset is the understanding that –

Failures are not personal, they happen because of circumstances. Rather than giving up on the goal, prepare better and persist until success.

Understand your limitations and break big goals down into smaller, achievable tasks. Celebrate each achievement to show your mind that it's evolving and enjoy it.

<u>THE 3 BASIC STEPS TO FOLLOW:</u>

- **BELIEVE YOUR IDEAS**
- **FOCUS ON YOUR GOAL**
- **CLARITY**

BELIEVE IN YOURSELF: Appreciate yourself for the fact that your mind is creative enough to generate ideas or eager to learn new ways to achieve your Goals.

At the same time it is equally important to allow yourself to believe that something might not work, this attitude lets your brain start saving energy and you don't dedicate yourself 100% on things that do not work.

Celebrating small victories is essential and encouraging to get where you want.

FOCUS: Focusing your priorities and completing the other tasks later – it simply means not wasting your energy on what cannot be resolved at the moment.

CLARITY: Gain clarity about your role in the business, your target audience and focus on what you do best. In addition to special effort you must also be able to delegate responsibilities.

By implementing these advices into practice, you will be able to get more results with less effort and can save your energy to achieve your goals faster!

II

NEW PERSPECTIVE

"We have never witnessed so much access to information on our fingertips yet sometimes we are unable to find out the -Secret Sauce; but we find it until it is the only option"

With the ongoing rat- race competition in all streams, exploring the new level of creativity and critical thinking has become a part of everyone's daily routine.

However, the perspective of continuous growth even during the situation of uncertainty, demands to focus on the development of certain proven psychological training of thoughts that can identify new opportunities, flexibility, able to see changes before it happens and more confidence to move towards growth.

(1) In the process of establishing a business, entrepreneurs can handle the highly uncertain environment by acquiring positive emotions.

(2) Positive emotions affect the formation and expansion of key activities of entrepreneurship

(3) In the process of entrepreneurship, emotional stability is a performance dimension, parallel to business growth.

THIS PROVIDES A NEW PERSPECTIVE TOWARDS ENTREPRENEURIAL JOURNEY!

Start-ups are often the main source of economic growth in emerging economies; encouraging entrepreneurship is a strategic policy for the majority of the countries. Hence, **BEING AN ENTREPRENEUR IS ONE THE BEST FEELING I MUST SAY!**

However, you may have already come across a situation where you need a little extra pinch of Creativity to be added to make your product or service stand out among the crowd. You would have strived hard day and night to think of that **ONE UNIQUENESS** that your product/service can provide for it to dominate in the market or to make it the best in the market.

Sounds familiar?

So our goal in this Book is to share what the main characteristics of the entrepreneurial mindset are, so you can succeed in your business —whether it's taking advantage of qualities you already have or nurturing those virtues.

III

THE WINNING MINDSET

"ENTREPRENEURS ARE DOERS NOT DREAMERS"

In a busy and competitive society, defeats and victories begin to build inside each person—and mind power is the starting point for self-improvement.

We are born with exceptional traits & characteristics inbuilt in us, as we grow every minute, every second has valuable teachings beneath the actions

& responses but only few can uncover these & treasure them with a positive mindset.

"We are what we think. With our thoughts we make our world"

- Buddha's phrase seems true than ever

If we think that our mental and cognitive abilities have been accumulated over an evolutionary history that has lasted millennia, it is not difficult to see their importance in what constitutes the individuality of each person and how this individual relates to the world and to the other.

Mind is one powerful god's gift anybody can ever ask for! All we are expected to do is to nurture it with good ambience & encourage learning more & more. The sooner we understand the hidden secrets of **MIND**, the faster we achieve our **GOALS**!

IV

THE IMPORTANCE OF MASTERING YOUR MIND

Your thinking is the basis of your decisions and consequently, of your destiny. So, controlling your mind is the most direct way to influence events and adapt in the best way to the unexpected.

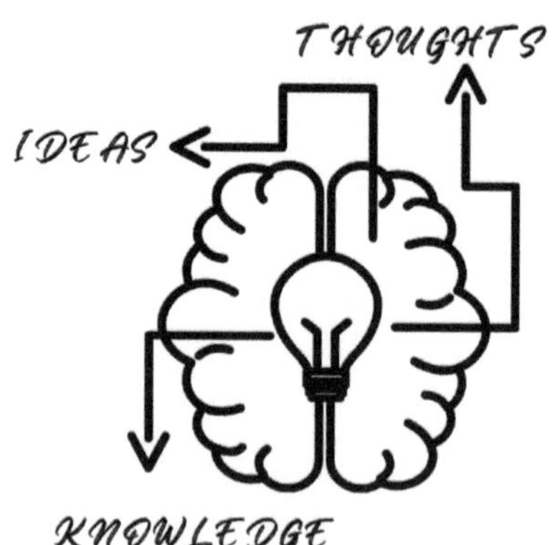

With this mastery, in addition to thinking and planning better, you can start to have a different attitude towards life and business, which results in less suffering and more happiness. This feeling comes from understanding your purpose and how to go about achieving it. Your achievements will be nothing more than confirmation that the path followed is the correct one.

It can be said that controlling our thoughts is as important as controlling the body's movements, because from them are born the feelings and thoughts that can cause us great pain or raise our potential to the height where our dreams and goals are.

You are

SMARTER

than you think!

Once you know how our mental gears work, it becomes possible to direct your operation towards self development and the achievement of your dreams and goals. The limits of each person depend only on their will and personal effort.

Another gain is related to performance: the more the mind is actively used, the more misunderstandings and weakness in the face of behavioural addictions decrease considerably —which means an increase in personal efficiency that will be impossible to go unnoticed.

Therefore, it is no exaggeration to say that mind control is at the base and directly influences your prosperity, profession, career, education, health and quality of life. Your thoughts are the starting point for achieving personal and professional evolution and for making the world a better place by **HELPING OTHERS** and by providing **VALUE**.

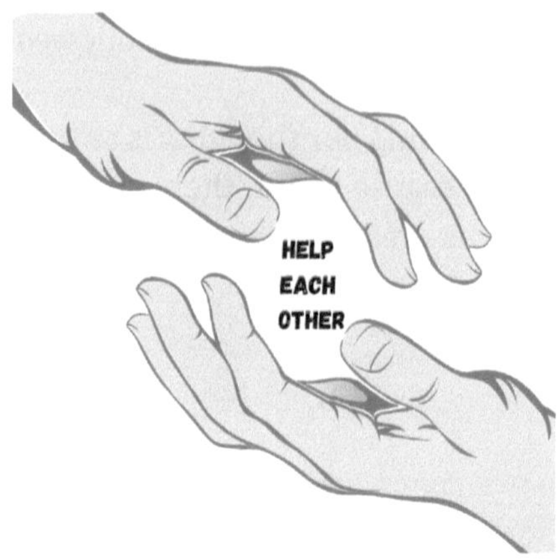

Faced with an issue so important to our lives, many scholars and scientists have been dedicating themselves to understanding how our minds can work in the best possible way, what are the factors that influence this functioning and the results that can be expected.

Let's begin listing down the easy steps to master thoughts and present you with the tips and information that will help you strengthen your mind and, consequently, be a mindful Entrepreneur who not only understands his/her strengths but also acts appropriately according to the scenario that ultimately results in profit, in addition to pointing out the achievements that come from mastering your ideas and desires.

There are some of the methods to get better results & these methods are effective enough to change the perspective of one's way of looking at situations.

Come on? Read on!

V

POWER OF MASTERING

Surprisingly, each individual have already been gifted with this power, but some realise it soon. There are certain proven methods, habits and effective ways to gain better results, cultivating positive thoughts and greater clarity.

Let's focus on some of the effective steps to inculcate for a better result personally and professionally.

1. DETOXIFY YOUR MIND

Of course, it is not easy, and perhaps bordering on impossibility, to filter 100% of our thoughts. It is a fact that our emotions often conspire against us. In other situations, it is the co- existence with other people, with different points of view and approaches to life that influences us.

There are situations, where negative thoughts are all around. But we need to be firm in absorbing only the positive thoughts and let it get **"SEEDED"** and find room to grow in our mind. They end up being the root, gaining strength to your life. These habits represent a healthy mind, gain of value time and high efficiency in your productivity, as your mind uses a large amount of energy to save them, turning into a peaceful state.

2. FILTER YOUR THOUGHTS

The second step, as with any improvement process, is to start organizing your mind. This means, in the first instance, separating what is useful from what is unnecessary and what is harmful.

Being selective about how do you devote your time and mental effort guarantees the possibility of using your capacity, in the topics that will bring the best return to your life & avoiding the accumulation of unnecessary 'debris'.

As you manage to predominantly cultivate positive thoughts, this will tend to be reflected in other aspects of your existence, from your imagination to your experiences. This is because the mind has a creative capacity, that is, what we think or imagine finds ways to manifest in the real world.

That's why it's so important to cultivate positive thoughts over negative ones. If a negative idea arises in the mind, we must immediately replace it with a positive one.

EXAMPLE: Considering the worries as **"The LESSONS" of LIFE** and tuning your mind into thinking only about the solutions for the problems and steps to move ahead with your life in the path of Success.

3. SEEK TO HAVE A QUIET MIND

As we implement these good practices in our daily lives, we discover other ways to deal with our mind, based on our personal characteristics and circumstances.

In order to clearly see these points of improvement, it is important to cultivate the habit of **MENTAL CLARITY**, that is, to avoid as much as possible the continuous and disorganized flow of thoughts.

When you feel that your mind is cluttered, look for an activity that can help to organize it:

Listening to good music,
Time with Nature,
Spending quality time with loved ones,
Meditating,
Breathing exercises to relax,

Anything that makes you Happy

Gradually, these practices will lead you to the conquest of what is called **"QUIET MIND"** thoughts free from disorder and restlessness and a steady imagination, capable of getting rid of the usual disturbing thoughts, deceitful feelings, the confusion of ideas and ineffective choices.

A quiet mind is able to observe thoughts and mental movements, in a detached and dispassionate way, as if they occurred outside of its own consciousness. No matter how difficult or complex it is, it will not shake the tranquillity of someone who has conquered this condition.

4. SELF-CONFIDENCE

The state of constant improvement and improvement of thoughts is the most effective path to reach mental power, as we have seen so far. On the other hand, this state of mind must be balanced with a fundamental characteristic to be successful in the practical world.

That's because, without a dose of it, it's impossible to start any activity, at the risk of getting stuck by insecurity. A confident state also encourages positive responses from those around us.

Thinking more about how to reach your goals is always more effective than focusing on the difficulties in starting or finishing a task.

5. CULTIVATE GOOD THOUGHTS

The best way to keep your mind away from getting caught up in bad thoughts is to make sure it's already occupied with better ones. Cultivating positive ideas and feelings is the fastest way to strengthen your mind and deliver real results in your life.

Doing so helps us to develop a more optimistic outlook, live in a more humorous frame of mind, and achieve our goals. Good thoughts need to be sown, cultivated and, at the right time, will bear fruit, in the form of the results that the person starts to reap.

In short, to change your visible reality, you need to change the invisible one that exists in your mind.

"GOOD THOUGHTS PRODUCE GOOD RESULTS"

6. REVIEW YOUR THOUGHTS PERIODICALLY

To ensure that you are on the right path and that the previous steps are well consolidated, it is essential to make regular reviews. After all, this is an essential step in any improvement process: everything always starts with an initial analysis, a diagnosis, and, as the project moves forward, new revisions are made.

It is through them that we can verify if the planning is being applied correctly, if the results are being satisfactory, if there are directions to correct and how this can be done in the most effective way.

When it comes to a journey to mastering your own mind, regularly examining your thoughts can be the difference between the success and failure of your efforts.

The discipline to monitor our thoughts, review our ideas and, eventually, correct directions is the certainty that we are cultivating a new mental model, which may be the way to achieve a better future and greater personal happiness with our achievements and individual reality.

VI

BENEFITS OF MASTERING THE ART OF MINDSET

The benefits of having greater control over your mind are varied and important, and can be divided into 2 groups:

- **The Harm you Avoid**
- **The Benefits you Get**

In the first category, it is getting rid of feelings such as stress, anxiety and fear, which, if left unchecked, can result in serious illnesses such as depression and panic disorder.

It is one of the important steps to address certain issues at the earliest and divert the mind to focus more on improving the mindset.

In other words, a controlled mind brings with it mastery of emotions, balance, growth in empathy, greater tolerance, improvement in self-esteem and self-confidence, by gaining clarity about the nature and mechanism behind your thoughts, you will be able to fully control your mind & easily free yourself from ideas and reflections that make you suffer. This skill will enable you to focus on what really brings **VALUE TO YOUR LIFE!**

In this Chapter we were able to understand the basics of nurturing the Mindset; in the next Chapters we will discuss more about the psychological point of view to get the utmost clarity on training your Mind.

Find some of the best proven methods to train your Mind naturally that can re-build your thoughts helping you immensely directing your subconscious mind work for **YOU** and **YOUR BUSINESS!**

Doesn't it sound exciting? Then, let's meet in the next Chapter!

VII

PSYCHOLOGICAL PEEK

The emotions, moods, or feelings of entrepreneurs that accompany the entire process of entrepreneurship play a vital role. As an important psychological feature of entrepreneurs, it is important in optimizing entrepreneurial cognitive ability, inducing entrepreneurial behavior and then entrepreneurial performance.

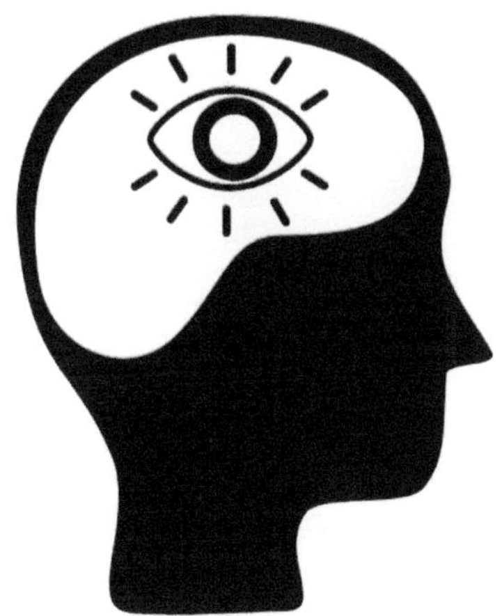

Psychological state of an Entrepreneur can influence many aspects of their life. It may be Cognition, motivation, energy, the self-concept, creativity, interpersonal behaviors and the activities of entrepreneurs can influence the results of their businesses. That is, the problems, personality traits, states and family history can affect both the personal functioning, as well as the operation of their businesses.

These are various phases that an Entrepreneur goes through the process of his/her ability and work pattern; & how the emotional variations impact on his/her business!

The entrepreneur's work is commonly known as quite stressful, as these professionals are subjected to various pressures, risks, many hours of work, and so on. Some researchers have been concerned with studying the general mental health and well-being of these professionals.

Some studies involving the mental health of entrepreneurs reported that these professionals experience certain issues with the mental health.

Aspects of successful personality in entrepreneurs have also been shown to be associated with a greater number of anxiety and stressful conditions in everyday business. Some also go through hard times of psychiatric conditions as anxiety, such as fear of failure that can alleviate the impulsiveness.

VIII

THE MODE OF EMOTIONS

Each Entrepreneur has their own approach towards the process of their Entrepreneurial levels. They all realize that they are enjoying different experiences brought by entrepreneurship, which makes them happy and satisfied in the process of work. This stage overflows with excitement and happiness.

Amongst them, fear, anxiety and depression also stand out and are the main highly aroused negative emotions.

Fear comes mainly from uncertainty.

For example: As an Entrepreneur, before the launch of products/ services, entrepreneurs often question whether the chosen entrepreneurial path is right and cannot predict whether and when the existing investment will be rewarded.

In addition, entrepreneurs are happy with product launch and are eager to know feedback from others after the product is officially launched, it can test their past efforts and clear assessment achievements.

Therefore, most of the emotions described by entrepreneurs are positive and negative depending upon the acceptance of the result.

We know that happiness is the ultimate goal of human behavior and the real essence of behavioral motivation.

People make rational choices to maximize their enjoyment. The happiness based on the realization of individual self-worth is greater.

The emotional state in decision making may affect the judgment and results of entrepreneurs differently; well-being can improve the initiative of entrepreneurs by establishing psychological resources.

So, ultimately the more active entrepreneurs are, the more it's easier to adhere to the entrepreneurial activities.

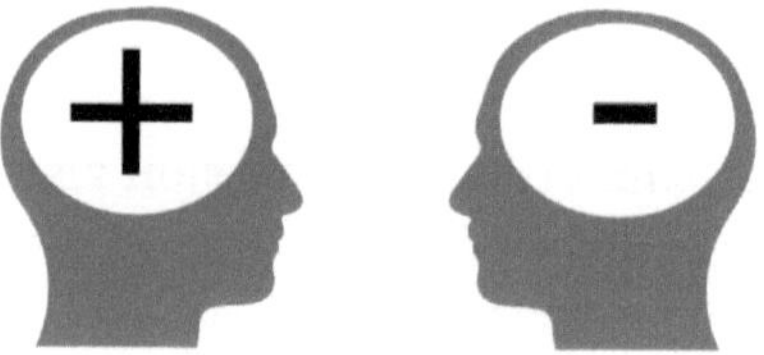

However, Entrepreneurs are bound to experience different emotional fluctuations in various stages of entrepreneurship

IX

COMMON BELIEFS VS TRAINED MIND

In this process, entrepreneurs constantly experience new things and obtain recognition, bringing in highly aroused positive emotions. Entrepreneurs are faced with a high degree arousal of negative emotions caused by an uncertain environment and setbacks. To persist in this phase, entrepreneurs should take actions to eliminate the influence of negative emotions.

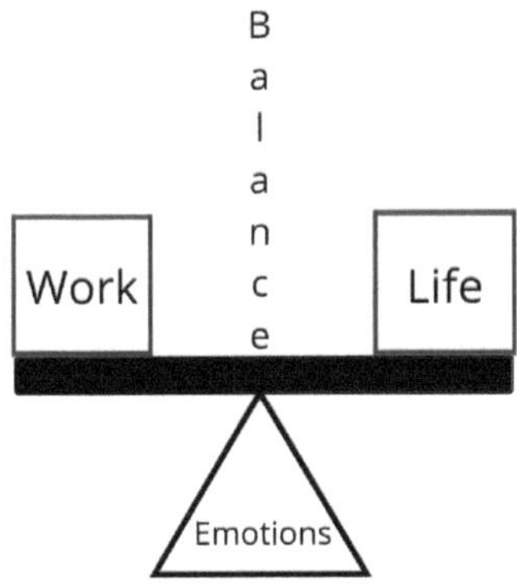

Here is an overview of how to train the Mind to look for more opportunities rather than pondering upon Negative thoughts.

ENTREPRENEURIAL STAGE

PRE-LAUNCH STAGE

GOAL

(1) Establish entrepreneurial team

(2) Focus on short-term goals; prepare to launch products and services

EMOTION (COMMON BELIEFS)

Positive emotions: excitement and joy (experience new things and get support) Negative emotions: fear and depression (environmental uncertainty, lack of resources, and support and criticism)

BEHAVIORAL STRATEGIES BY A TRAINED MIND

(1) Acquire support and recognition from family, friends and other relevant personnel

(2) Selective feedback

(3) Use this stage as a process to accumulate experience

LAUNCH STAGE

GOAL

(1) Launch new products and services

(2) Review and reflect on the entrepreneurial process

EMOTION (COMMON BELIEFS)

Positive emotions: excitement and happiness (positive feedback after product launch; success) Negative emotions: depression, confusion (negative feedback or failure after product launch), boredom and tiredness (repeated tasks)

BEHAVIORAL STRATEGIES BY A TRAINED MIND

(1) Review and reflect on the entrepreneurial process and engage in the past to bring positive experience

(2) Redefining the cause of entrepreneurship and taking the process of entrepreneurship as a process of learning and growth

POST-LAUNCH STAGE

GOAL

(1) Optimize existing product services or launch new products
(2) Consider enterprise growth

EMOTION (COMMON BELIEFS)

More frequent feelings of positive (success) and negative (failure)

BEHAVIORAL STRATEGIES BY A TRAINED MIND

(1) Engage in past successes
(2) Launch new products and services
(3) Seeking broader support and recognition

X

TYPES OF MINDSET

In an Entrepreneurial journey there is no absolute systematic solution for each level of situation and scenarios, therefore we need to analyze and discover the possibilities before we consider Entrepreneurship as a career option.

There are two types of Mindset:

- ***CLOSED- MINDSET***
- ***PROGRESSIVE MINDSET***

<u>CLOSED- MINDSET</u>

- **CHALLENGES** - Avoid Challenges
- **MISTAKES** - Make excuses or give up easily/ consider it as an end of the road
- **EFFORT** - Effort is limited to just major issues
- **CONSTRUCTIVE FEEDBACK** - Ignore feedback
- **SUCCESS OF OTHERS** - Feel insecure

PROGRESSIVE MINDSET

CHALLENGES - Embrace the Challenges
MISTAKES - Persist in the face of Mistakes
EFFORT - Effort is essential on every task
CONSTRUCTIVE FEEDBACK - Learn from feedback
SUCCESS OF OTHERS - Find lessons and Inspiration from other achievers

An Entrepreneur Mindset is actually critical to success and to rapidly changing world, as we begin to dive-in deep into this subject we realize that not only can we nurture it but also train our minds effectively.

"THE COMBINATION OF ENTREPRENEURIAL and ARTISTIC SKILLS creates WONDERS"

But what matters the most is how skilled or well versed are we in solving problems, finding opportunities to find our **SELF REFLECTION!**

Yes and this is the **KEY** factor to prove our ability to move ahead in the path of Success!

XI

BALANCING MENTAL HEALTH AND SUCCESS

Entrepreneurship is all about seeking professional success through innovative work. Therefore, the idea is that entrepreneurs are courageous and constantly motivated people, who are always engaged in new projects and determined to achieve their professional goals.

We know this is very true and real. However, enterprising people often face numerous challenges that, if not well managed emotionally, can ruin everything!

There are numerous factors that contribute to imbalance the emotions of those who opted for entrepreneurship. The pressure for results, the hours of sleep exchanged for work, the concern with financial returns and the eagerness to make everything happen quickly and without mistakes... All of this can harm the mental health of those who decide to change their life by undertaking.

RELATIONSHIP BETWEEN MENTAL HEALTH AND ENTREPRENEURSHIP

Many people understand that undertaking is synonymous with taking risks. Even if it is to reach a new professional level and become a good "boss of oneself", the entrepreneur, in fact, needs to be ready to deal with unexpected and extremely challenging situations.

Due to insecurity, especially at the beginning of a project, entrepreneurial people are usually more susceptible to stress, fatigue and anxiety.

Depression is also another great enemy of entrepreneurship. It usually appears in the face of unforeseen scenarios or periods of financial difficulty that entrepreneurs – whether they are owners of small or large businesses – are liable to go through.

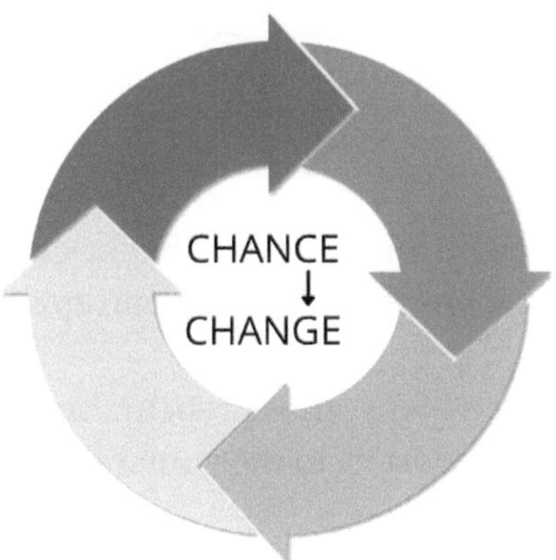

Thus, the relationship between entrepreneurship and mental health is very close, with the entrepreneur, in a way, dependent on the fluidity and quality of their emotions to achieve their goals and carry out their projects and be ready to change their perspective of handling situations.

XII

TOPICS THAT REQUIRE IMMEDIATE ATTENTION

Before we jump on to know the strategies to take care of the emotions, let's understand the main reasons that affect the entrepreneur's mental Health.

There are some reasons why entrepreneurship is related to emotional problems, and that should alert us to the vulnerability of entrepreneurs and care for their mental health.

Let's look at some examples:

IDENTITY FUSION:

"You are your Company"

This statement is widely heard in the world of entrepreneurs and often causes entrepreneurs to end up losing their personal identity in exchange for their corporate identity.

This behavior tends to generate an existential void because he cannot dissociate himself from the figure that represents a brand, he can develop an identity crisis.

But this can be managed well with the thorough expertise in having the right mindset and balanced emotions, I am here to help you more on this in the coming chapters.

GREATER LOAD OF RESPONSIBILITIES:

Along with entrepreneurship comes a huge list of responsibilities that fall on those who choose to own their own business. The list of tasks of an entrepreneur, who cannot always delegate function to the team, is endless, and this usually generates a high load of stress.

When all this responsibility is not well managed, the entrepreneur is more prone to mental fatigue and emotional overload, which reflect on the accomplishment of the work and the success of the enterprise.

ACCESS TO HEALTH RESOURCES:

When it comes to mental health, the case is even more serious. Not to mention that though there are many effective campaigns to publicize the importance of taking care of emotions; right sources are still not available to many entrepreneurs.

The reality is, unfortunately, entrepreneurship is hampered by the absence of benefits such as the health plan, which employees with a formal contract usually have.

And as at the beginning of a business, financial resources tend to be scarcer, most entrepreneurs do not hire a health plan and do not think they should invest money in it, even though they know the need to take care of their emotions and seek treatment.

LACK OF GUARANTEES:

Unlike someone who has a steady job, with a salary on the scheduled date, and all the rights and benefits that are guaranteed, the entrepreneur has to deal with an absence of guarantees, especially financial ones.

After all, not all returns will depend exclusively on the effort put into making the business work. There are many variables that involve entrepreneurship and determine the success – or not – of those who follow this path.

This sense of vulnerability and constant uncertainty about the future is responsible for causing anxiety in many entrepreneurs, especially those in the early stages of a project.

SOCIAL ISOLATION:

Due to all the dedication needed to make a new business take off, it is quite common for the entrepreneur to spend more hours of the day at work, missing family moments and weekend events with friends.

Thus, social isolation ends up being an unplanned consequence, which can substantially affect the mental health of entrepreneurial people.

It is also quite common for individual micro-entrepreneurs (MEIs) to work alone, causing them to lose the bond with colleagues and creating a solitude, which even voluntary, can end up generating a feeling of loneliness and sadness due to the lack of contact with other people.

XIII
DEALING WITH EMOTIONS

For all the reasons presented and a series of reasons involving entrepreneurship, it is necessary to pay attention and care to mental health, before the lack of control of emotions jeopardizes the progress of business and forms a barrier that prevents the entrepreneur from achieving professional success.

3 STRATEGIES FOR SUCCESSFUL ENTREPRENEURSHIP

Below, we list some strategies to take care of emotions that are extremely beneficial to entrepreneurs:

PROMOTE SELF-CARE

Forget the old "I work too hard, I don't have time for this" excuse. You need to find a way to take care of yourself, as the lack of attention to yourself can have serious consequences and put a loss of all investment – of time and money – in an undertaking.

Therefore, find some time in the middle of the daily rush to practice a sport or physical activity that is pleasurable. Pay attention to the things that bring happiness outside of work, and consider leisure time as sacred as corporate obligations.

And above all, take a vacation! Plan your professional life as an entrepreneur so that you can spend a period away from activities, resting and replenishing your energy. Only then will the continuity of the projects be fluid and will run faster towards success.

SEEK SELF-KNOWLEDGE

Practicing self-knowledge is the main strategy for those seeking to take care of their mental health and have greater control over their emotions.

This makes psychotherapy a great ally of entrepreneurship and makes it possible to develop the ability to manage crises and solve problems with more assertiveness.

Among so many challenges and uncertainties in the life of an entrepreneur, there are also benefits that cannot be lost along the way. For this, it is necessary to know how to manage feelings consciously, to understand how they affect your routine and what can be done to avoid or exclude negative interferences.

KEEP YOUR SOCIAL LINKS

Attention: We are not talking about the network! On the contrary, keeping in touch with people beyond work matters is essential when you want to feed feelings of well-being and productivity. Surround yourself with like minded people who often talk positively and motivate you to achieve your Success.

Your connections with loved ones increase happiness and ward off feelings of loneliness, as well as significantly decreasing your chances of being affected by depression. Thus, the tip is to always cultivate friendships and bonds, without forgetting, of course, romantic relationships.

Although many people believe that having a relationship with someone can take the focus and distract attention from important things (work), on contrary it is true that healthy relationships tend to contribute even more to the smooth running of business and be a stimulus for the pursuit of objects of those who undertake and most of them are able to grow their business with immense focus and stability.

XIV

IMPACT OF RIGHT MINDSET

When talking about entrepreneurial success, many people focus on talent, perseverance, creativity, financial foresight, and people management.

NEW MINDSET

Let's say you have a great idea and hired the right people, gradually made a few smart financial decisions and stuck with your plan.

All these elements play a role, but there's one overriding trait often missing from the discussion.

THE ENTREPRENEURIAL MINDSET

If you start a business from scratch, you'll know that every step along the way, a certain mindset is required. Various thinking patterns accompany every decision, action, and plan.

Most of us aren't born with the right entrepreneurial mindset. Most characteristics are cultivated over long periods and often learnt through trial and error. Entrepreneurial routes vary, but over time, most successful business owners would have developed a certain attitude.

The impact of the right Mindset plays a vital role in the growth of the business!

How do these thinking patterns result?
Let's dive in!

1. *UNDERSTANDING THE POWER OF HABITS AND SMALL WINS*

Most successful enterprises are nothing more than an accumulation of small wins. A few sales here, a new client there, and these seemingly minor gains aggregate into a well-oiled machine.

This rule applies to businesses as well. As an example, try to make one more sale this month, one more the next month, and so on. If your business usually makes 100 sales a month, that's a 12 % improvement in a year. Most business gurus would consider 12 % a respectable growth rate.

"We are what we repeatedly do. Excellence then is not an act but a habit."
—Aristotle

I know, one sale might not sound like much. In a small enterprise, however, the improvement represented by one sale can make a big difference over time.

Once you are tuned into the right Mindset, you would be often looking out for -the next challenge! That would be to identify the habits that will generate these small wins. What can I do regularly to make one more sale each month?

Once you've found potential small improvements, we will be more focused on building habits that will secure them.

Consequently, one of the most powerful impacts of an entrepreneurial mindset is the verve to build habits that will spawn continuous improvement.

2. PERSONAL GROWTH AND UNDERSTANDING THE WORLD AROUND YOU

We are aware that if we want to cultivate an entrepreneurial mindset, we need to understand ourselves and the world around us.

In this sense, personal growth and entrepreneurship go hand in hand. By working on yourself, you'll learn how to improve your skills, ideas and plans into your business.

Reading, taking on new challenges, and delving into your character will help your entrepreneurial ventures in many ways. By challenging yourself with personal growth experiments, you learn about your fears, hopes, and strengths.

As an example, meeting people with entirely different backgrounds will help you identify your social talents and shortcomings.

Constant personal growth endeavours will also further your confidence in your abilities. You'll become attuned to your expertise and learn how to acknowledge your failures.

This self-knowledge will enable you to understand and value others. By embracing your strengths and faults, you'll be better at handling other people's flaws and fortitudes.

Consequently, a zest for personal growth and social insight would be prime sectors of your entrepreneurial journey.

This appetite for personal growth will help you utilize your talents to the fullest. By highlighting your areas of expertise, it will also pinpoint the activities to focus your energy on.

3. TIME MANAGEMENT AND PRIORITIZATION

As entrepreneurs, our most valuable resource is **TIME**.

We need time to let our creativity flourish, to manage our finances, and to put our long-term vision into action.

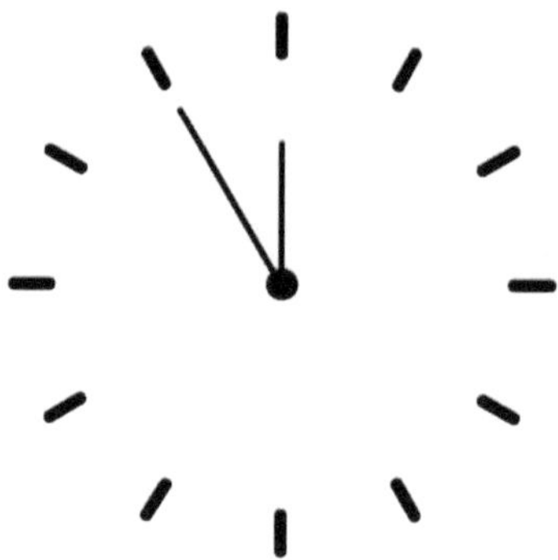

According to this theory, we should attempt to get our chores done with the least possible effort — freeing up space for more meaningful tasks.

We need to focus our time and energy on business-advancing endeavours. Our entrepreneurial mindset needs to be in a state to recognize productive and unproductive activities to implement it the right way.

To nourish your entrepreneurial mindset, try to determine what activities, clients, and ideas have the most impact. Direct the bulk of your time and creativity toward those activities.

By creating clients and jobs, you will be able to create more high-profile clients.

Prioritization allows us to dedicate more time and energy to the most high-paying, main Clients/target audience.

4. FOCUS ON PROVIDING VALUE INSTEAD OF CREATING WEALTH

"Entrepreneurship does not equal wealth it equals to providing more value and solving problems"

Entrepreneurship, demands a different approach with the right Mindset. In very simple terms, you start out with an idea and a plan.

After a while, you will be able to turn it into a **PROFIT**. If your business continues to grow thanks to its valuable output, you'll attract more customers. And if your products and services do well in the long run, you can make truckloads of money.

As an entrepreneur, your wealth will be the result of a long-term process. It is rarely an instant perk of entrepreneurship. Hence, the right Mindset lets you geared up towards providing value to customers and not creating wealth in the short term.

If you're solely interested in creating wealth, you're an investor, not an Entrepreneur!

Of course, investors can make tremendous gains thanks to luck and financial decisions, but this is not entrepreneurship.

If entrepreneurship is your calling, providing value to your customers is the - **KEY TO SUCCESS.**

You'll build a long-term business instead of a short-term investment.
"THE MORE VALUE YOU PROVIDE, THE MORE YOU GET BACK"

5. MONEY MANAGEMENT

Any business needs proper financial management to grow, survive, and prosper.

As a newbie entrepreneur, creating wealth should not be your first concern. Managing your finances, providing value product and services, on the other hand, should be basic.

In the context of an entrepreneurial mindset, you should never lose sight of the financial part of your endeavours. No matter how passionate you are, you are still running a business.

Most entrepreneurs, start ups fail in their first year.

Yes, this is often the result of expectation mismatches and untimely work ethics, but it's mostly a case of bad financial management. Managing your finances the right way is mandatory from day one, right attitude and mindset assures that you work on a systematically equipped business plan and be focused on long-term goals — both financially and growth-wise.

Your expectations will remain realistic; & your mindset will have a proper balance between financial intelligence and ambitious creativity.

6. LONG-TERM VISION

Entrepreneurship is a long and windy road. Though you fail, you can still reposition yourself constantly.

To navigate unavoidable bumps along the way, you need a long-term vision.

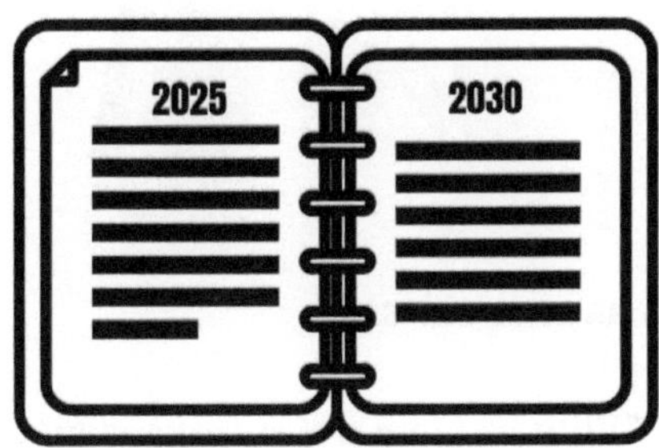

To turn your ideas into a lucrative online venture, you'll need to assess the market, evaluate your competition, analyze the best niches, and devise a growth strategy.

All of these elements are components of a long-term vision for your writing business.

Consequently, your right entrepreneurial mindset will not stop at talent, creativity or innovation.

It will include a vision — a puzzle combining different pieces that will turn an idea into a profitable business in the long run.

7. BALANCING FREEDOM AND RESPONSIBILITY

Many want to become entrepreneurs to benefit from the freedom attached to having your own business.

The coin, however, has two sides.

"With freedom comes responsibility"

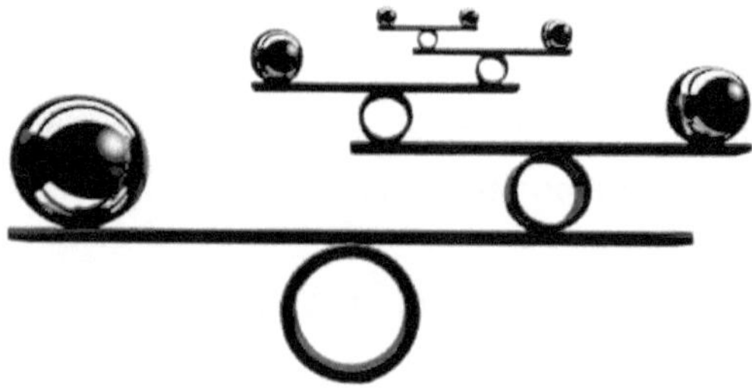

To adopt an entrepreneurial mindset, you need to consider every decision with their differences.

I have the freedom to invest $500 into project 'A'. In that same page, I will also bear the responsibility of losing $500 if project 'A' goes wrong.

The same goes for taking time off, hiring people, and paying yourself.

In this context, two attributes strengthen your entrepreneurial mindset.

>> First, you need to learn how to live with the endless contradiction of freedom and responsibility.

At the same time,

>> Capitalize on your freedom.

In a broader sense, using your freedom to advance your business — while at the same time managing your responsibilities wisely — will reflect a strong entrepreneurial mindset.

XV

HOW TO TRANSFORM YOUR MIND INTO A WINNING MINDSET

This is a **CHOICE**.

Mindset is nothing more than a belief.

These are powerful beliefs, but they're just something that's in your mind, and you can change your mind. Think about where you would like to go and what mindset can take you there.

In the field of mental configuration, one thing leads to another.

For example: The conviction generates different thoughts and actions. Likewise, if you believe you can change and improve, you will.

Being open to information about your abilities and limitations in order to learn will open up a world of possibilities for you. It just depends on how open you are to it.

There are two distinct worlds: the rooted characteristics and that of changeable ones.

In the first, success consists of proving that you are smart and talented. In the second, being successful is opening you up to learn something new.

XVI

HOW TO START THE MIND SHIFT

Every success story is marked by ups, downs and a turning point. These people, one day, decided to act.

Obviously staying in the same place always seems more comfortable, but it's certainly not what will get you out of your current situation.

.

So ask yourself: Are you where you want to be today? Do your current conditions meet your goals? If not, move!

Find inspirations, look for examples of people who moved on, without giving up, and ended up conquering everything they wanted.

.

Most of the people you admire have a story of resilience to tell. Look up to them.

Also, believe in your potential. If the source of inspiration managed to get where they wanted to, why can't you too?

People will always try to discourage you, so it is necessary to trust your ability and competence.

Even if they tell you that "you can't", that "you can't do it" and that "it's not possible"

DON'T GIVE UP!

Once you find your Inspirer, the inspiration and believing in your potential, it's time to take advantage of the opportunities that come your way.

You will feel afraid, you will feel challenged, but you will embark on an endless journey of self-knowledge.

This process will give you a chance to clearly recognize what your strengths and weaknesses are.

The beginning of change can only come from a clear and objective view of oneself. With this awareness, the possibility of success is much greater.

.

So, do you prefer to have a progressive mindset?

Let's find out how?

.

With a progressive mindset anyone can develop a skill or broaden their intellect if they put in the effort.

And the more effort, the better you can become at what you want.

.

People with a progressive mindset value learning. They have a strong belief in transformation and the power of dedication.

Optimism is one of their main qualities, they think that everything can always get better, and they strive for it.

The fact of trying and never giving up, and more than that, learning from each of these mistakes, turns positivity into your greatest virtue.

.

They often rely on hard work and value merit rather than just the result. Practice, training and methods are the motto of progressive mindset people.

For them it is important to see the positive points of the process and understand how to correct the negative points.

They are constantly working hard to reach their goals, if it is to learn something new, they create a study plan and follow the established schedule until they reach the expected result.

In the professional field, they seek to overcome their limitations and improve their knowledge daily, they are not afraid to take on new responsibilities and are even excited about the opportunity.

They are not discouraged when they make a mistake, they think that, if there was a mistake, there is a need to review the process, and they still see this as a possibility for improvement and to make an effort to reverse the situation.

SETBACKS AND DIFFICULTIES

They see difficulties as opportunities to learn about the weaknesses and understand how to develop them.

Obstacles and external setbacks do not discourage them. The motto is: Failures are an opportunity to learn, so whatever happens, you will win.

CHALLENGES

Challenges are extremely exciting for anyone with a progressive mindset.

Challenges are opportunities to develop, excel and learn new things. Embrace the challenges, because you know that you will come out stronger on the other side.

INTELLIGENCE

Understand skills and intelligence as the fruit of effort. Believe that the brain is like a muscle that can be trained and therefore that intelligence can be developed. This mindset trait is a motivating factor and leads to the desire to learn and improve more and more.

EFFORT

Effort is seen as the path to personal and professional growth.

There is no wasted effort, because you either conquer or you learn. Effort is necessary to grow and master useful skills.

PERFORMANCE

As they seek knowledge and learning consistently, in addition to constant performance and performance reviews, these people reach ever higher levels of achievement. As they improve, they create positive feedback that encourages them to continue learning.

SUCCESS OF OTHERS

Success is not seen as a game where, for one person to win, the others have to lose.

The success of others is a source of examples and **INSPIRATION**.

REVIEWS

Negative reviews are very helpful as they are sources of information.

They don't see negative feedback as something personal, but as a success meter of their current abilities.

XVII
EXERCISE YOUR MIND

The brain works like a muscle, that is, it becomes stronger as it is exercised and stimulated.

"A powerful mind, as long as it is under the control of its owner, makes it possible to achieve exceptional results"

Most of the possible ways to increase your mind's capacity are quite accessible and depend more on discipline and focus than anything else.

We have listed some of them below:

READING

It's the best exercise for the mind. By reading good books, you learn and dialogue with other powerful minds and increase your repertoire of skills, thoughts and ways of reading and understanding the world.

We usually hear that a CEO reads one book every month but in reality with the busy schedule, this is not possible to some of us, but it's **ABSOLUTELYOKAY!**

Yes! It's absolutely okay if you are not able to read many books but make sure to read at least one book in 6 months.

Sounds fair?

The best option is to follow your Motivator/Inspirer (option- social media, books & business websites), understand their way of handling, addressing problems, how they find the solutions, how they come up with the new ideas, what are their strategies? What steps do they follow?

In this way your mind is in constant mode of learning and understanding the best ways. To your surprise - You are indirectly training your subconscious mind to reflect those solutions/ideas when you come across certain similar problems/hindrances.

As physicist Albert Einstein said - Each time your mind opens to a new idea, it will no longer return to its initial size — on the contrary: it will come out richer and stronger from this experience and ready to reach new heights.

This is the treasure that you can find in books and teachings from the right people.

GOOD NUTRITION

We are what we eat. Our brain needs about 20% of the energy and nutrients we consume, so the healthier and richer in fruits, vegetables & healthy meal in our diet, the better the quality of the "fuel" that supplies it.

On the other hand, a bad diet deprives us of essential substances for the proper functioning of the body. In this scenario, we end up becoming easy prey for diseases and, consequently, we compromise our well-being.

Healthy diet maximises your efficiency in utilization of precious time and mental energy the right way.

PHYSICAL EXERCISE

Regular physical activity helps increase brain function and also enables us to stay in the right physical health condition.

"A healthy body is the ideal space to reach the mastery of the mind"

As the absence of physical illnesses and the feeling of well-being allow it to concentrate the energy and good feelings necessary to reach another mental stage.

It is literally the translation of what the ancient people already preached:

"A healthy mind in a healthy body"

QUALITY SLEEP

Another essential component of the practices that bring health to our bodies and strength to our minds is sleeping well. When we fall asleep, it's like submitting our brain to a detoxification process, the famous detox.

During sleep, we regenerate cells, remove toxins and eliminate redundancies and useless information from memory. Sleep also reduces blood pressure, anxiety and restores energy.

Sleepless nights represent unproductive days and a blurred mind, making it very difficult to keep thinking about your goals and the positive values related to them.

Maintaining good habits, such as having proper sleep conditions, exercising and eating healthy, especially at night, are ways to achieve quality, restorative sleep.

POSITIVE THINKING

Having your mind attuned to good things decreases stress and anxiety, work on adding the fuel that avoids toxic thoughts and help to strengthen your self-control and willpower.

Thinking positive is mandatory, but being prepared for negative is a must!

Rather than looking for problems or reasons to complain about life

.

Invest your time in boosting your mental energy in ways to transform your reality towards growth both personally and professionally.

.

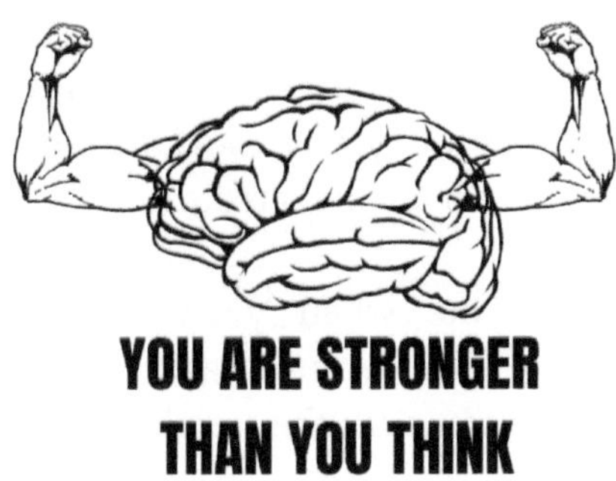

With this we come to an end of this Chapter,

Find the best proven methods, techniques & secrets to train your mind to gain the right mindset that lets you to achieve your goal much sooner and faster in the next Chapter.

I am so excited, can't wait to explain to you the proven methods, techniques and activities in the coming Chapters!

XVIII
THE GAME PLAN

At the beginning of an entrepreneurial initiative, everything is an adventure. It doesn't matter if you're working nonstop and completely stressed. You simply want to build and create.

But there comes a time when you've moved from ideation to management when your big adventure has become a job and that spirit of innovation can get buried under the weight of your day-to-day tasks. If you allow your energy to diminish, your organization stops growing. Before long, someone will outdo you.

"Right Entrepreneurial mindset will keep your company at the Top of its Game!"

This entrepreneurial attitude is not just about avoiding failure, though. It's about building a business that thinks creatively, scales efficiently and generates trust in consumers. These principles drive start-ups, and they can drive big businesses, too. It's just a matter of maintaining an entrepreneurial mindset.

"YOUR BUSINESS WILL EVOLVE IF THE LEADER DOES"

LEVERAGING THE ENTREPRENEURIAL MINDSET

Keeping up that mindset is about empowering your front line to work towards finding better ways to move your business forward — whatever "better" means for your brand in any given moment.

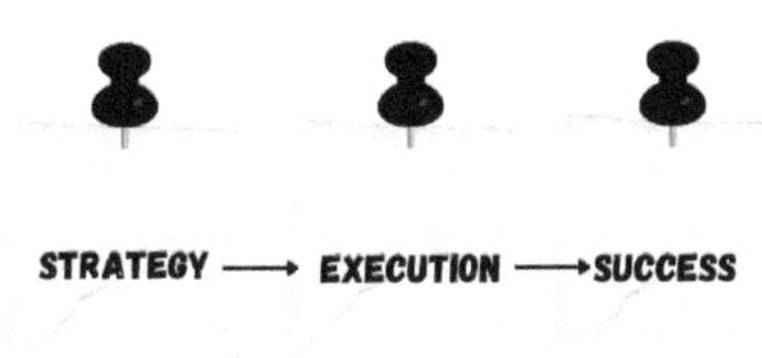

And this Entrepreneurial Spirit starts with - The Entrepreneur.

Admit that you have room for growth, too. Your business will never evolve if its leader doesn't. You can't possibly know everything it takes to reach your business's potential, so don't stress or burden yourself with all the tasks. Instead, ADAPT.

Not having all the answers is something every entrepreneur will face. You can keep looking at your problem with what you already know, or you can exercise that entrepreneurial spirit, thinking critically about what's missing in your dilemma and what are the new ways and how you can achieve it.

When a business needs the utmost support during the growing phase, it will be in need to implement serious changes in light of this rapid growth that demands to be completed immediately. During this whirlwind period, employees often ask you what should be the next step.

And being an Entrepreneur you didn't really know because every stage of growth brought new challenges that you never faced before.

Growing a business to scale gradually helps us to focus more on the process of business, operations, people, clients/targeted audience, growth and culture of business.

This gives you a game plan to move forward if you adapt to the changes!

ESTABLISH ROBUST SELF-AWARENESS

Don't let your title or accomplishments define you -- these attributes are shallow and short-lived. Resting on the "I'm the boss" principle inhibits your growth and, therefore, your company's growth. Rather, knowing your strengths and weaknesses gives you the tools to lead authentically and dynamically, making way for an entrepreneurial leadership style.

Many leaders struggle with self-awareness, but if you understand the concept of leadership thoroughly, you'll have a better understanding of your priorities, decision-making style, and communication skills -- and a better idea of what it will take to keep your business in constant entrepreneurship.

Your organization's progress is contingent on how well you, the entrepreneur, maintain and employ your entrepreneurial mindset. As long as you're willing to realize you have room for growth and grow accordingly & lead with strong self-awareness, you'll overcome one of the greatest challenges of being an entrepreneur

XIX
MINDSET SHIFTS TO SUCCESS

To change your mindset, you need to identify ways of thinking and acting that hold you back. This way, it will be easier to make the necessary changes for you to evolve and see the world in a different, improved way.

A person will only be able to change his/her behavior after he has managed to change his mind set.

Therefore, if your results are not satisfactory, you may need to make some changes in your mindset and, with that, change your behavior for the better.

To help you with this task, I will list some important tips below

1. VISION AND CLARITY

Vision and clarity is what the entrepreneur wants to achieve, what vision of the business he wants to develop.

Vision is accompanied by clarity, because it is necessary to see what you want and see it clearly.

For this, you need to set goals.

2. MAKE PLANS FOR YOUR LIFE

Making plans for your life is a great exercise to discover what needs to be changed in the way you think and act.

When you make plans for your life, in different areas (whether financial, personal, professional), you identify which thoughts and behaviours prevent you from carrying out those plans.

Thus, you can make the necessary changes in mindset and behavior, which is already the path to success.

3. PURPOSE

All people are driven by a purpose.

Those who do not have a purpose may do things for the sake of doing and may not succeed in anything.

People with purpose accomplish great things as they are focus driven.

4. DON'T PROCRASTINATE

Procrastination is a great enemy of those who are looking to develop a winning mindset.

You need to learn how not to procrastinate.

Learn techniques on how to beat procrastination.

You need to be someone of initiative, who doesn't "push things" that need to be done.

Having a clear vision and purpose will help you have a "**fuel**" to accomplish your goals and objectives, thus avoiding procrastination.

5. LEARN FROM YOUR MISTAKES

We are human beings and therefore we are flawed. When trying to achieve success, we are exposed to failure, this is normal.

But, what is not good is giving up in the face of a mistake, is keeping the focus on the mistake.

If you made a mistake, find out what happened and how you can learn from it.

One tip is to learn from the mistakes of others so you can save time and save time, energy and money.

6. FOCUS

Focus is the skill that makes you get things done. Without focus, you get lost and can't finish anything. Learning to focus is one of the skills a successful entrepreneur needs to have (or develop).

7. PRODUCTIVITY

Productivity is the ability to do more and more using fewer resources, especially time.
The entrepreneurial mindset seeks to be more productive in everything.

Studying and learning more about productivity will make all the difference in your journey.

8. HOLD THE OPPORTUNITIES

Don't let opportunities pass you by. Take advantage of every opportunity that arises, because you will hardly have a new chance to have the same opportunity.

If it seems challenging, dive into self-knowledge and discover the skills and competencies you have today, and what you need to develop. Don't be afraid; don't think you can't handle it, when a great opportunity appears. You definitely can.

9. LEARNING

Entrepreneurs need to be constantly learning.

Learning and keeping up to date to respond promptly to market changes is essential to succeed as an entrepreneur.

10. BE MOTIVATED BY YOUR FAVOURITE PERSON

To develop a successful mindset through behavior change, seek inspiration from successful people.

Successful people always have a history of overcoming. Study the stories of successful people, seeking inspiration to succeed too.

I'm sure that when you get to know some great entrepreneurs, you'll have enough motivation to move forward.

XX
OWN YOUR POWER

THE ROLE OF A DIARY

The most unique quality of writing is- we can express the best emotions onto a paper without any hazels, without any emotional barriers coming along the way. We can cherish the best achievements & consider the failures as a lesson.

All we need is to accept the fact that it is absolutely okay if we are not able to write down every day, all it matters is to stay true & let the thoughts pour in to an extent that you finally have nothing else to write on a certain thought or situation.

We have the power to turn ourselves into the best version of anything we desire or dream of, recollecting the best moments of life and career or even recording your good times, knowing or unknowingly influencing you to feel best about yourself! It directly tunes your subconscious Mind to feel good about yourself and feel confident from within.

Bonus Tip: Create a dedicated page to record your achievements; though it is tiny little one or a major one, some things can motivate us without our knowledge, the conscious mind often strives hard to come up with an end result after a long conversation & conflicts happening inside, this is time the subconscious mind embarks a strong & firm self confidence. You can feel it for yourself! So, come on begin to record & narrate your best version now

HOW TO HANDLE NEGATIVE SITUATION

As a business owner we come across certain positive and negative situations. At some point or the other, situations can often challenge us in an absolutely different dimension that could make us go through good times or bad times.

Well, have you heard of **BALANCED EMOTIONS?**

Yes, that's the answer! But now the question still remains how to do it?

Well, here's the catch – The sudden uncovering of an outcome that does not fit into the boundary of our existing & inbuilt thought process has a huge impact on us. The role of training the mind becomes a priority, let's understand the fact that- the protocol of nature is- no matter whether we accept or not; nature will either create miracles or create disasters.

Thinking positive is mandatory but being prepared for the worst is a MUST!

Now, similar to the process of nature, our lives and careers/professions are also the process of positive & negative outcomes and it's assured to happen. Why not be prepared mentally?

The change that occurs every moment is unstoppable, therefore being & responding to certain events of life logically makes more sense both for self & to the business.

TRUST THE INSTINCTS

Have you ever noticed the first thought you get as soon as you come across a person, thing or even a situation?

Now Instincts are the first thought we get when we face a situation, the later ones are manipulated from the process of our thoughts. Often the first thought is ignored by most of them but these instincts prove to be the most relevant & accurate solution or response to consider.

Trusting your instincts can be your ultimate way of self trust!

Believe me you will be able to focus more on other important sectors rather than spending your valuable time on thinking & re-thinking about one problem or situation.

These instincts will definitely have a message in it & with no dilemma you can certainly trust these that direct us to the have some facts in hand to move ahead in the business.

EXPLORE NEW OPPORTUNITIES

We all know that- *"If opportunity knocks the doors, then we invest time & energy in building a house"*

Exploring new opportunities can mean both personally & professionally.

We need to call ourselves destined to be born & brought up in the era of Digital Evolution to its greatest level, where every tiny little work can be completed within fraction of seconds with the help of technology and software platforms.

A step away from our comfort zone would discover our hidden talent; this not only improves our skills but also broadens our mind to look up for more opportunities.

PROVE YOURSELF

Understanding the concept of failure!

Failure is a sure stepping stone that upturns the eagerness to search for an opportunity. Many tend to dishearten themselves when they come across failure but actual failure is when you don't trust yourself at the time when you need yourself the most! Hard phase does not last long so cheer up right away!

The best way to stay motivated is to celebrate **small WINS**, instead of waiting for the big deal to happen.

You can celebrate the joy of that little success you come across because the happier you are, the sooner you will find ways to succeed.

If we shift our perspective a little, failures seem to be preparing us to change our thoughts, tune a little, and create some more strong walls across our objectives so we are equipped enough to handle & manage them in a way that results more favourable to our **GOALS**.

Problems & failures are part of the journey called **LIFE**. The sooner we find the way to jump start, the better life we have!

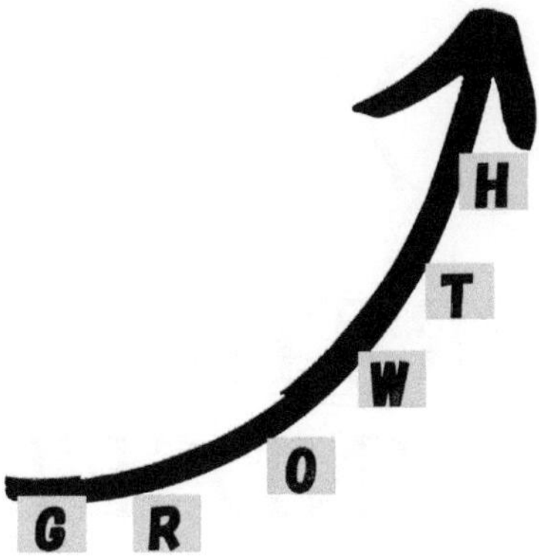

Always remember

"AFTER FAILURE RISE LIKE A PHOENIX"!

XXI
MASTER THE DIGITAL MINDSET

With a drastic change & so many technological advancements, the digital mindset emerges, and it couldn't be different.

The digital mindset refers to the technology-oriented mindset. And, for those who want to succeed in such a competitive market, they need to adapt and develop this mindset.

.

As an entrepreneur, it is essential to develop this mindset, so that whenever a new technology comes along, you are open to learning and using it in the best way to ensure that your business does not fall behind.

.

Now you already know that it is possible to change your mindset, and how to take the first steps,

.

I will give you 5 precious – and very simple – tips on how to develop a success mindset.

UNDERSTANDING YOURSELF BETTER

You must know which features you like the most about yourself, but what about the ones you like least?

.

- What are your weaknesses?
- Are you impatient or anxious?
- Do you procrastinate?
- Are you afraid of making mistakes?
- Are you angry with yourself or with others?
- Do you have a negative self-image or are you overconfident?

These questions help to know the perception we have of ourselves. Consequently, it directs us to paths that can improve negative aspects and open us to new possibilities.

It is necessary to explore your weaknesses and face your flaws in order to become strong and powerful.

UNDERSTANDING WHERE YOU ARE

You need to identify what stage you are in.

Do you know what your current status is?

Take a moment, reflect on your life, and identify where each aspect of your life is at.

Ask yourself:

- What job am I in?
- What position do I hold?
- Do I like what I do?
- What is my relationship with my family?
- What is my relationship with myself?
- Am I, at this moment, chasing my goals and desires?

If you want to change the way you see the world and act, this is where your journey begins.

UNDERSTANDING WHERE YOU WANT TO BE IN FEW YEARS

Now it's time for you to imagine what you want accomplished.

Give shape to your goal; create in your head the image of these goals achieved.

Project your mind to the moment when your goals are a reality, and feel what that will be like for you.

Close your eyes and start identifying your purposes, where you want to go in the short, medium and long term, and what strategies will be used to achieve these purposes.

It is an exercise in imagination, but one that will take you to the desired future.

UNDERSTANDING THE LEVEL OF WORK

Now, it's not enough to wait for the results to appear, right?

Obviously, when the objective is understood, it becomes a driving force in the quest to achieve it.

But getting there will take dedication and persistence.

Persistence is the difference. It is a skill that can be developed and cultivated. Pursuing something we want helps a lot to keep that necessary fuel to move forward.

What drives us to achieve things is our desire. However, at this stage, action is critical.

So take the ideas off the paper and put each one of them into practice.

It's a similar idea to a race:

There will be times when you think you won't be able to continue, but if you get over that breathless moment and the wear and tear, you start to recover and start visualizing the finish. Just don't give up.

UNDERSTANDING HOW TO STAY MOTIVATED

The world is a box of temptations, seeking to have our attention at all times, calling us to something new, something different, but which often doesn't add us to anything.

But it's no use being aware of who you are if you don't have the motivation and focus necessary to achieve your goals.

For starters, it's very simple: take a pen and paper and start describing everything you would like to achieve and that gives you pleasure. Make a list or a step by step.

Don't stop in front of other people's impossibilities, fears and opinions, this is your assessment and it matters **ONLY to YOU.**

Think of things you enjoy and invest in them. This will make it much easier to stay focused.

"The Secret to stay focused is to celebrate your small wins, the happier you are, the sooner you will find ways to succeed"

- Mrudhula Ravi Kiran

XXII

PROGRAM YOUR MIND FOR DIGITAL ERA

From clothing, food, accessories, automobiles, events to education, almost every sector has transformed their business to digital platforms; it has almost become mandatory to shift the offline business to online if we need our business to stay on the scale of profitability.

Don't you agree?

Well, to do so we need to understand & have basic knowledge and information about the opportunities that exist online, the various platforms & software technology available to extend the hands of an Entrepreneur to stay updated as well as stay competitive enough in the market with the right technological methods.

Feel overwhelmed?

Don't worry I am here to help you!

These mindset shifts are important & have been proved to have immense results in being a digital entrepreneur.

YOU ARE WHAT YOU THINK, SO THINK BIG!

Initially, you can test, research, evaluate and make improvements to your project. You're just starting out and nobody starts big. Human beings are like that, aren't they?

We were born babies and we grow until we reach the peak of our talents.

.

And, what is the purpose of it? What's the point of starting small? You will test your initial ideas...did it work? Accelerate funds and invest, to increase results. And, in case it didn't work out, you can make adjustments in the strategy, because you haven't invested heavily yet.

BEGIN WITH WHAT YOU HAVE

Initially, you can test that some people think that starting an online business takes a lot of investment.

And no, it's not necessary! You can start with what you have on hand.

A computer with internet access makes it possible to get started & a decent amount of Investment is all it requires in the initial stage.

.

Evaluate everything you need to get started in the simplest way possible. However, that doesn't mean you shouldn't charge yourself.

The important thing is to initiate and put into practice your ideas for the business

YOU ARE THE CREATOR OF YOUR WORK

We are conditioned to the mentality of the worker, where we are part of a larger system and we contribute with our tasks, and someone decides for us what we have to do on a daily basis.

.

In entrepreneurship it's not that, because in this case, you decide everything. And that can be a blessing or a curse. Only depends on you.

.

You may simply decide not to take the necessary actions, sometimes out of laziness, procrastination, busying yourself with other tasks, or for any other reason. Or, you can decide to work hard, and it's not just another job, but your life's work.

OVERNIGHT FAME

One of the biggest things that digital entrepreneurs give up is anxiety for short-term results.

We want everything overnight. But, things don't work that way.

Look to the future, the results are in the long run. In the short term, we work to build what will bring us the result we want.

In the short term, you may not have any financial results, but there are other metrics that you need to analyze, such as the generation of traffic to your website, the increase in the number of leads, the growth of your email marketing list.

Celebrate the growth of these numbers, as they are the ones that will bring the future financial result.

LEAD AS A LEADER

Even if you only work in your company, be the leader for yourself.

Leadership is a behavior, not something we were born with.

For some people, leadership is something we are born with. But I believe in a culture where people become leaders through their daily effort & yes we can learn a lot from such successful leaders.

When your company starts to grow, you will need employees, and the best way to lead them will be by example. That's how I built my company, through the best leadership style that exists and daily I dedicate myself and reap the fruits of my business.

They will see in you an example to follow, inspire them and everyone will win.

BE ACCOUNTABLE

Take your responsibility. A business is something very serious. Many people who start a digital business don't really see it as a business, and that's a big mistake.

Take responsibility for the success of your business, just as a company president does.

But what is taking responsibility?

Being responsible is nothing but balancing both the profit & loss. Accept & agree with the result, you need to either strive hard to move forward or celebrate the win to move ahead. Do the same with your business.

Take full responsibility for your business, and its success or failure.

GAIN COMES WITH DISCIPLINE

Disciplined work is the good old recipe for success. It's no use forcing yourself to work in one day, and spending two, three days doing nothing. Work must be disciplined, consistent and taken seriously.

You may not be the most talented, but discipline will bring out a lot of talent in you. Want to see an example? You may not have any talent for recording videos, and talking to the camera may seem impossible to you. But, try to start, and proceed. Go recording videos and see in three months how your videos will be. Evolution will be something remarkable.

And everything has to be like that for a digital entrepreneur. Do as many times as necessary for you to achieve the best result.

MISTAKES ARE COMMON

Mistakes are common and what to do when they do?

The right time to test and fail is when we are starting our business.

Don't worry about mistakes now; they will be your best teachers.

Be prepared to learn from your mistakes. Don't beat yourself up, really learn. You must keep persisting, take each error and do an analysis of what happened, fix it and move on.

Adapt to the mindset of continuous improvement. It will always be possible to make improvements in your business.

MONEY MANAGEMENT

This is a concept you cannot forget: your company has expenses that you must manage. And an "expense" is not really an expense, they are investments or reinvestments.

Reinvestment is nothing more than part of your income that you will allocate to reinvest in your business, putting into practice the concept of continuous improvement.

The basic concepts as we all know:

YourProfit = **Revenue – Expenses – Reinvestment**.

Note: You need to be very careful to avoid unnecessary expenses in your business.

Adapt this mindset from the beginning; make sure to check your expenses periodically & there is reduction in expenses.

XXIII

BUSINESS AS A SYSTEM MANAGEMENT

It is important that you understand that your business is a system, as a whole. Let's compare our body.

Can you work well when you have a headache or backache, for example? No we cannot! So, if one part of my body isn't working well, the rest isn't working well. And that happens to your business.

You need to see your business as an interconnected system. If something is not working well, the whole system will be compromised.

And what happens when the system works perfectly? That's more & more joy! There can be sales and more sales.

Therefore, you need to take care of each area of your business, because, like our body, they are all important to stay healthy.

ACTIONS ARE WORTH MORE THAN THE IDEAS

Do you know why? Ideas alone don't change anything, but actions do.

We often think about that brilliant idea, to create something new that will revolutionize the market. This is very rare for a person to have a brilliant idea.

However, no matter your idea is not as much as brilliant but still you can always get ideas from the thorough market research, once that happens, take the necessary actions that your business needs. Plan, study, invest, act and grow!

Within your planning, make a To-Do-**List**, which is a to-do list of the things you need to do in your daily life. Go through the tasks done and evaluate the results.

WIN YOUR CUSTOMERS

It's not what we want to do and develop that determines what people buy. You need to find out what people want, and deliver an answer to them through a digital product. That's how you can sell a lot.

Keep your focus on delivering valuable content to your customers. This is a very important lesson, because people buy what they see value in.

And when you deliver interesting content to your target audience, with relevant information, your audience will see value in what you offer.

XXIV
THE SECRET OF MANIFESTATION

A Glimpse of manifestation,

Every time we establish a purpose in life, we want it to be fulfilled in the shortest possible time. Depending on the size of the goal, dedication and our mental map, the time in which that purpose will be achieved can be varied.

There are people who master the manifestation process very well, that means that they are capable of believing in their natural capacity for creation, they have a contagious optimistic character that allows them to take advantage of incredible opportunities.

You set your intentions. You made your vision board. You're using positive affirmations. You're trying to see and believe with all of your heart that you simply have a replacement $10,000 client calling you up and handing you a check for your services.

You've been doing this for years, but your business remains not where you would like it to be.

.

When an idea passes from the mental pace to the physical pace is known as the manifestation process, this process helps to maintain a positive attitude and thinking creative most of the time.

.

There is no doubt that thought is powerful, those who are always waiting for the best in life manage to build a very effective expectation, so a person with the gift of master manifesting with an entrepreneurial mind, will have thoughts and actions that will lead to achieve their goals faster.

.

The entire material world and the conditions that surround a person are the product of the level of vibration that exists in the quantum field, in that sense, those who learn to control their mind, always focus on the ideas that bring them great well-being, then it is possible to raise the frequency in the quantum field, thus the manifestation will be accelerated and the creative energy of the universe will be able to give a spectacular impulse to those ideas.

.

We are creative beings, but it is difficult for us to become aware of it, this process takes some time and also be able to control all the ideas that cause suffering:

Suffering is created in our own mind, manifestation is able to block negative ideas and emotions that limit power, because we need to have well-being and joy so that ideas bear the fruits we hope for, internal happiness is our best ally and the foundation of Personal Development.

.

So you have to make efforts to make that happen,

.

It is possible that we are going through some difficulties, but if we insist with ideas such as: "I am wonderful", "life gives me the best" etc. Even if those ideas are not there, your affirmations will be able to manifest them.

I'll be sharing some of the powerful ancient secrets with a few added steps which will take your manifestations from feeling like you're chasing rainbows to you receiving what you truly desire for your business faster than ever.

Here's my step-by-step guide to manifestation for business owners in order that you'll experience the enjoyment of manifestation and make your ideal, prosperous, and super, satisfying business.

CLARITY OF INTENTION

This initiative is according to most manifestation practices. To be ready to receive anything, you've got to be clear on what it's that you simply want to receive. Therefore, what you are doing here is start working with an intention list.

Write down all of your intentions in the present tense.

Example: I sell out my next projects with ease and appreciation.

Writing down your intentions is super powerful, but if you would like to pack an additional manifesting punch, make a vision board. Find pictures that symbolize the essence of your intentions and make a collage with them.

FEEL PRODUCTIVE

Now this is often where the practice gets pumping with extra power. The law of attraction states that – 'like attracts like'. Basically what this suggests is that your feelings attract more circumstances into your life that assist you feel an equivalent way that you are feeling.

Since your feelings are so important, you've got to get what it's that you simply want to feel once you fulfil your manifestation.

After you recognize what you would like to feel by having your manifestation come to fruition, consider a minimum of 3 other activities you'll do to feel an equivalent feeling that you simply desire. Then schedule those activities into your calendar in order that you'll feel the sensation you would like to manifest and attract more of it.

Example: I feel satisfied when I: gain financial freedom / complete an outside workout / Finish a book.

GRATITUDE

The last step is a daily practice of having a feel called - **"GRATITUDE"**

This is a blend of gratitude and meditation. Every morning, take a walk and offer gratitude to everything you see and feel. This may start your time off with a sense of gratitude and an acknowledgement of the reality of how you are feeling.

Example: Thank the Universe, thank everything & everyone you see and come across every single day, thanks for giving me exactly what i want, thank the profession you are in for being an expert.

Do these three steps consistently and watch your entrepreneurial desires manifest at a speed together with your constant efforts and consistent work.

XXV

KEY SECRETS TO MASTER YOUR THOUGHTS

There are numerous leaders and entrepreneurs who have spent more than 2-3 decades searching for the ultimate personality trait to achieve success.

1. PERSISTENCE

Persistence has a vital role and stands out, it is the key to turning wishes into reality — People can discipline their mind and thoughts by developing the skill of Controlling your Mind.

A persistent person is not frightened by difficulties or failures. On the contrary, he/she takes advantage of the lessons learned to resume stronger and more experienced projects. Much of what we face in life is the evidence of endurance rather than ability.

2. CONFIDENCE

Confidence is the trait that lets you know what you want. Equipped with this feeling, you are able to use your skills and resources to achieve your goals.

For people with low self-confidence, change is only possible by overcoming paradigms, mental models that are built from childhood. Therefore, gaining confidence depends on a good ability to analyze and master thoughts.

The understanding that each person's boundaries are much more mental than physical and the ability to change the pattern of those thoughts is the foundation of transformation through self-confidence.

3. POWER OF ACTION

THIS IS THE CHARACTERISTIC THAT SEPARATES DREAMERS FROM ACHIEVERS.

It's about overcoming fears, barriers and resistance to moving from idea, plan, to practice — it's our ability to "get into the field" to make it happen.

Almost everyone has plans and purposes that have remained shelved or postponed in one of those procrastination rituals we know so well.

Mind power, however, is able to break this procrastination cycle. This paradigm shift is a direct result of your ability to make thoughts work for you rather than against your goals.

Once in motion, the path becomes real and confidence grows. As a result, new goals, achievements and course adjustments naturally arise in order to reach the objective of their work.

Goals, by the way, are an important tool for achieving mind control. By setting really challenging goals, worthy of their potential, and continually thinking about them and how to achieve them, a person starts programming his mind for success.

This is because we end up becoming what we think about most. That way, keeping your goals in mind often tunes your imagination to what you want to achieve and keeps your brain focused on positive things.

4. ATTITUDE

This is probably the most important trait for success. It is the key, the starting point to walk the path of personal and professional fulfilment.

Attitude is at the base of your decisions, including the decision to go in search of improvements in your life. The other qualities we have can be pale if there is not the necessary attitude to put them into practice.

A controlled mind will find it easier to exercise a positive attitude towards life and its projects. It is from there that the whole flow of changes and achievements that lead us to achieve our goals and dreams is born.

XXVI

7 PILLARS OF THE ENTREPRENEURIAL MINDSET

We have listed seven most important pillars for you to awaken your entrepreneurial side

WRITE THE UNDERLINED WORDS ON A BOARD / SHEET;

READ THEM EVERY SINGLE DAY TO WITNESS THE CHANGES IN YOU!

TRUST

"I AM CONFIDENT"

Confidence in yourself! This is a watchword that must be kept at all times. People may disbelieve your designs, but you? Never!

COURAGE

"I AM OPTIMIST"

Facing challenges and problems is quite common in any business, being prepared to turn those problems into opportunity without fear is all that matters, makes any entrepreneur, whether small or large, a distinguished entrepreneur.

VISION

"I LOOK BEYOND THE FRAME"

Those who undertake a different look, as they can see beyond, can imagine situations and circumstances that did not even happen and avoid any unforeseen events.

LEADERSHIP

"I AM A LEADER; I GUIDE MY TEAM TOWARDS SUCCESS"

The leader is the one who transmits all the confidence and strength to those he needs to make his project viable. A good leader leads, without excess of authority, a team towards success.

COMPETENCE

"I AM DETERMINED TO MAKE IT HAPPEN"

Being competent is making it happen. This means not being afraid to work, to move ahead & prove your abilities until the project results in fruition. With focus and determination, the entrepreneur goes far and turns his business into a success story. This means giving up laziness, in addition to living only on that business until it reaches the desired level.

RELATIONSHIP

"I AM GOOD AT NETWORKING FOR MY BUSINESS"

Networking is critical to the success of any business. A good entrepreneur knows many people, is influential and articulate. The more people are part of the mail, the better the reach.

LOVE

"I AM COMPLETELY IN LOVE WITH MY WORK"

It's no use playing in a business thinking solely and exclusively about money. Loving what you do provides greater involvement with the investment, greater creativity, dynamism and willingness. If you put love into your business, you're more likely to do well.

Now that you know what the best ways to become a successful entrepreneur are, how about taking that filed project out of the drawer and moving on? Remember that it takes a lot of dedication, and above all confidence that your idea will be a success.

XXVII

ACHIEVE YOUR GOALS

With the constant search of techniques and methods available around us, with a strong intention of finding impactful procedures on achieving our goals with flying colors of success, we work hard day and night with a hope of looking at our future more happily with our loved ones.

The ultimate result that we often focus on is the **CONVERSIONS** using the systematic way of helping our client/ targeted audience get their results.

It definitely demands hard work yet smart work blended with fears, emotions and curiosity.

LOVE YOUR IDENTITY

Now, that's the best line I can tell you! Yes, you heard me right!

Be proud of being an Entrepreneur, it takes an immense amount of dedication and a strong mind set to even think about becoming an **ENTREPRENEUR**!

"ENTREPRENEURS ARE GAME CHANGERS"

So, buckle up! Being an Entrepreneur is the best decision you have taken in your life!

The path that we take as an Entrepreneur has beauty of its own! Every professional or every phase of life is submerged with challenges of their own, no job or professional is a piece of cake to walk through.

The only difference of being an Entrepreneur is:

YOU OWN YOUR BUSINESS!

YOU ARE THE MASTER OF YOUR BUSINESS!

Wow! Isn't that an amazing feeling!

This Amazing feeling of Entrepreneurship should compel you to get up and get going every single day to achieve your dream of **BECOMING A SUCCESSFUL ENTREPRENEUR!**

You know your **GREATEST ASSET** is **MIND** so,

"BEGIN TO MAKE YOUR FOUNDATION STRONG AND BUILD AND EMPIRE OF YOUR BUSINESS NOW"

VALUE ADDITION

The more you focus on providing value to your clients/ customers the easier it is to stay in their good books, to make them return back to you for more value. Work on creating irresistible offers that your business prospective **CAN NEVER IGNORE!**

Ok then, let's jump into a small activity:
Take a paper and answer to these questions:

- **What is my product/service all about?**
- **How can I provide more value to my customers?**
- **What are they looking for?**
- **How can I help them solve their problems?**
- **How can I help them to solve their problems quickly but effectively?**
- **What systematic sales process can I Work on?**

I hope that you have answered these questions, if yes! Take a look at your answers now, that's the simple marketing technique you will be using for your business.

CREATE THE RIGHT ENVIRONMENT

Work on creating an environment of positive results, well we know that success is inevitable, so create an environment that compels you to take actions you need to take to get that desired results for your business. We are bound to emotional attachments and the state of being the happiest can be one of the strongest reasons to achieve your goal.

Let's jump into another small activity:

Now imagine yourself on the other side of your achievement, imagine the day you have already achieved your goal of being the most successful Entrepreneur, with financial security, financial abundance, your loved ones are proud of you, you can see that happy spark in their eyes for you - Feel the ultimate happiness within!

Isn't it an amazing state to be?

Now write down the answer for these questions–

- **What steps did you take to achieve this?**
- **What made me achieve this?**
- **Who is my inspiration?**
- **What is my everyday thought that compelled me to get up from the bed and start working?**
- **What strategies helped you?**
- **What determination led you to achieve this?**
- **What sacrifices did you have to make?**
- **How long did it take to achieve this?**

Read the answers again and again!

THIS IS THE BLUEPRINT OF YOUR SUCCESS!

XXVIII

WITNESS THE NEW YOU

With the increasing sales and marketing techniques, creating strategies within a business structure, we tend to notice what I call "Entrepreneur uniqueness moments".

These moments reflect our approach to our professional life, and how we position ourselves within the huge competitive market.

As the trend changes so does the requirements so we wonder if we should continue to repeat our old strategies or if we would better reinvent our ideas of approach.

In the process, we decide to reinvent ourselves. We try to participate in various activities and networking, which take place constantly.

So I believe that this transition process will never stop, as it is continuous and necessary. You can't settle down and get stuck to one plan because you believe you've already reached the top, the maximum.

But this is the moment you feel you are transforming your mindset and reinventing yourself.

EXACTLY!

Mind is amazing but we have been in an impression of restricting it with some limitations. But NOW it is possible to find a way of doing, spend time and understand your capabilities.

Be different and take a different path from what the rest are used to taking, child-like eagerness is one of the keys to find new ways to be different. Challenging the norm just to learn from others and from our failures is courageous.

Entrepreneur Mindset helps discover they can make this world a better place, a career that's fulfilling and meaningful and be self reliant, it helps them to discover their passion and interests, achieve success remarkably today and continue being successful even in future.

"MAKE A MARK IN THIS WORLD"

YES! YOU CAN DO IT!

THANK YOU

I would like to thank you for your decision of opting for this Book; it means the world to me!

Thank you for investing your time and energy in learning. Hope this Book has served its best!

HOPE THE "NEW YOU" IS ALL SET TO PROVE YOURSELF WHO ATTRACTS SUCCESS, WHO THANKS GOD FOR THE WONDERFUL LIFE!

Wishing you good luck and Wonderful Success Ahead!
Regards
MRUDHULA RAVI KIRAN

www.ingramcontent.com/pod-product-compliance
Ingram Content Group UK Ltd.
Pitfield, Milton Keynes, MK11 3LW, UK
UKHW041851190726
13854UKWH00002B/843